THE SECRET SHRINE

The Secret Shrine

ISLAMIC MYSTICAL REFLECTIONS

edited and with photographs by
CATHARINE HUGHES

A CROSSROAD BOOK
THE SEABURY PRESS • NEW YORK

ACKNOWLEDGMENTS

Eastern Poetry and Prose, by R. A. Nicholson. Copyright 1922 by the Cambridge University Press.
Mystical Poems of Rumi, translated from the Persian by A. J. Arberry. Copyright © 1968 by A. J. Arberry. Reprinted by permission of the University of Chicago Press.
Readings from the Mystics of Islam, edited by Margaret Smith. Luzac and Company Ltd., 1950. Reprinted by permission of the publisher.
Rumi: Poet and Mystic, translated by R. A. Nicholson. Copyright 1950 by George Allen and Unwin Ltd.
Sufism: An Account of the Mystics of Islam, by A. J. Arberry. Copyright © 1950 by A. J. Arberry. Reprinted by permission of George Allen and Unwin Ltd.
The Tale of the Reed Pipe: Teachings of the Sufis, by Massud Farzan. Copyright © 1974 by Massud Farzan. Reprinted by permission of E. P. Dutton and Company, Inc.

Designed by Joseph Vesely

Library of Congress Cataloging in Publication Data

Hughes, Catharine   comp.
        The secret shrine: Islamic mystical reflections.

        "A Crossroad book."
        1. Sufism—Collected works.   I.   Title.
BP189.62.H83   297'.4   74-12106
ISBN 0-8164-2101-3

Manufactured in the United States of America

The wisdom and mysticism of the East have very much to give us even though they speak their own language which it is impossible to imitate. They should remind us of that which is familiar in our own culture and which we have already forgotten, and we should direct our attention to that which we have put aside as insignificant, namely the fate of our own inner man.

—Carl G. Jung

INTRODUCTION

The average Westerner is aware, whether vaguely or strongly, of the tradition of Christian mysticism: of John of the Cross and Teresa of Avila, of Augustine, Catherine of Siena, Meister Eckhart, Ignatius Loyola, and others. And, in more recent years, we have become increasingly conscious of Buddhist (especially Zen), Hindu, and even Taoist mysticism. Islamic mysticism—Sufism—the mysticism of such countries as Egypt, Iran, and Turkey, on the other hand, remains relatively unknown. Yet, Sufism, which has been called the "religion of the heart," is in many ways of at least comparable interest. It opposes worldliness; insists that the love of God is the major element in religion and that the principal means of achieving it is through contemplation and asceticism; and holds that "the religion of love is apart from all religions. The lovers of God have no religion but God alone." It was an Islamic mystic, Hasan al-Basri, who reminds us to

> beware of this world, for its hopes are lies, its expectations false; its easefulness is all harshness . . .

and another, Muhammad himself, who observed:

> When you see a person who has been given more than you in money and beauty then look to those who have been given less.

In *Sufism: An Account of the Mystics of Islam,* the Islamic scholar and translator A. J. Arberry describes Sufism as "the mystical movement of an uncompromising Monotheism." For, unlike some Eastern religions, that of Islam teaches that God is One, possessed of no equals. But he is not a "savior" in the Christian sense, for "salvation" is a question between the individual and Allah, the One Lord. A few, however, have been called to be his prophets, called to carry his unvarying message to mankind. They are not in any sense to be the subjects of worship, however. They are men—men who have been endowed with special Grace, men to be imitated and revered, men to be listened to.

For the Muslim, the Koran, a book of revelations to the prophet Muhammad, is the principal vehicle for this message. It is also, as Arberry writes, "the supreme authority to which the Muslim mystic looks for guidance and justification."

Muhammad was born at Mecca in A.D. 571, a son of the aristocratic tribe of Quraish. According to Arab historians, his parents, 'Abd

Allah and Amina, though noble, were impoverished. His father died even before Muhammad's birth, his mother when he was about six. When he was twenty-five, the future prophet married a wealthy widow some fifteen years older, whose business he looked after, at intervals going off to the hills for periods of meditation.

When he was approaching forty, Muhammad underwent an experience that launched him on his prophetic mission. It came in the form of a voice telling him to "Recite in the Name of thy Lord," and advising him that he had been called to prophesy. For a time, there were no further revelations, no further messages from the Lord. But eventually another did come, telling him to "arise and warn" his fellowmen. From that time forward until his death in 632, Muhammad regularly heard that same voice, held to be that of the angel Gabriel, and each time repeated its revelations to his followers. They were in time compiled in the Koran ("recitation"), with its admonitions and accounts of the prophets, its rituals and legal ordinance, which confirmed rather than supplanted the revelations of God through such earlier figures as Abraham, Moses, and Jesus.

It is not possible to establish precisely the origin of Sufism, though some historians date its major importance from the ninth century and its "golden age" as beginning in the tenth. The word "Sufi" itself seems to have originated as a nickname: The early ascetics in the Arab countries, living in poverty, wore garments of *suf* (wool)—for which they were criticized on the ground that, although Jesus had worn wool, Muhammad had been satisfied to wear cotton.

Al-Hujwiri, author of the oldest Persian treatise on Sufism, *The Unveiling of the Veiled,* wrote that "Sufism does not lend itself to any particular definition with words; the whole world, therefore, is its interpreter," and it is virtually impossible to define its Way to Reality or to reduce its doctrine to conventional Western terms. According to the Sufis, it is Love, not any sexual instinct or drive for power or similar factor that is the motivating force of life. Although man was at one time in complete harmony with the Absolute, he became separate and, now, apart and alone, he unconsciously longs for a return to his former union with reality, with the Truth. It is, however, a reality not to be found through thought or analysis, but through feeling. The mystical poet Jalal al-Din Rumi, many of whose reflections appear later in this book, wrote:

> The dryness of your lips is the indication of a need for water. This thirst is a splendid and auspicious experience, and the desire to quench it will take care of any obstacles. . . . Then there would be no need for any means or ways in the journey toward the Truth.

Sufi mystics believe that if a man can have the experience of a direct relationship with God he must himself possess a share of the Divine Nature, that the soul is made to mirror God's splendor, and that all things share in the Divine life. But in order to have such an experience the individual must be purified of self-love and sensuality. Only then can he attain the vision of God.

For Shaqiq of Balkh, the characteristics of the true Sufi could be described as: "First, freedom from any anxiety for one's daily sustenance; second, sincerity of action and a pure heart," and it is these sentiments that appear time after time in the writings of the Sufi mystics, almost without exception.

In its orthodox form, Sufi mysticism was first described by Harith b. Asad al-Muhasibi, a teacher said to be one "whose arrow attained its mark," who asked:

> What have you to do with delight in this world? It is the prison of the believer and he does not rejoice in it nor find pleasure in it. The world is only an abode of affliction, a place of care and sorrow, as Adam said: 'We were begotten of God, as the offspring of God, and Satan has taken us captive through sin.' . . . It is only when you come to appear before God that you will know the truth of the matter and whether God is pleased with you or not, and this alone is of consequence to you.

The similarities to the ascetic ideal in Christianity, with its doctrine of self-renunciation and surrender to God as steps to redemption, are, of course, obvious. There were, however, other, more individualistic, manifestations of Islamic mysticism, which displayed distinctly pantheistic traits. Abu Yazid al-Bistami, who died in 875, for instance, shocked his orthodox brethren with the proclamation "Glory to Me! How great is my Majesty." His brand of mysticism was not uncommon among the so-called intoxicated Sufis, and al-Hallaj, called "the Carder of consciences" because he reputedly could read the thoughts of men, was crucified in Baghdad in 922 for heretical pronouncements that included the assertion "I am the Truth." Yet another Sufi mystic is reported to have pointed toward himself, announcing, "There is nothing inside this coat except Allah."

But the mystical consciousness is often paradoxical, at times contradictory. The man who says "I am God" tells half the truth, the other half represented in "I am not God." There is what Walter T. Stace, in *The Teaching of the Mystics,* refers to as "not simple identity with God but rather identity in difference," and it is undeniably a significant element in Sufism.

Sufi, and especially Persian, mysticism produced several poets of distinction, and Jalal al-Din Rumi (1207-1273) is almost without question the greatest of them. Born in

Balkh, he made a thorough study of Sufism and for many years devoted himself entirely to mysticism. (It was Rumi who was responsible for the foundation of the Maulawiya Order, which had monasteries throughout the Ottoman empire, but is best known today for its circular sacred dance, whose participants came to be called "whirling dervishes.")

Rumi's extraordinary *Mathnawi* ("The Poem of Rhyming Couplets") is said to have taken some forty years to compose and encompasses virtually every aspect of Sufi speculation in an impressive blend of anecdote, wisdom, and humor. In images reminiscent of the great Spanish mystics Teresa of Avila and especially John of the Cross, its opening lines describe the Sufi mystic's plea to God:

Hearken to this Reed forlorn,
Breathing, ever since 'twas torn
From its rushy bed, a strain
Of impassioned love and pain. . . .

'Tis the flame of Love that fired me,
'Tis the wine of Love inspired me.
Wouldst thou learn how lovers bleed,
Hearken, hearken to the Reed!

Although Rumi was the greatest poet of Islamic mysticism, he was far from the first. Rabi'a al-'Adawiya (c.713-801), described by her biographer as "that woman who lost herself in union with the Divine, that one accepted by men as a second spotless Mary," is one of the most appealing, despite her austerity. Like Teresa of Avila, she kept her feet firmly on the ground even in the midst of her eloquent, sometimes soaring, espousal of the "pure" love of God, epitomized in such reflections as: "O my Lord, if I worship You in hope of Paradise, exclude me from Paradise; but if I worship You for Your own sake, then do not withhold from me Your eternal loveliness."

Legend has it that as a child Rabi'a was kidnapped and sold into slavery, then set free because her master recognized her as one of God's elect. She was the subject of numerous marriage proposals, but declined all of them, insisting that marriage was "for those who have a phenomenal existence" and that she had passed beyond this. "I have ceased to exist and have passed out of self. I exist in God and am altogether His. I live in the shadow of His command. The marriage contract must be asked for from Him, not from me."

Rabi'a is generally credited with having voiced the first Sufi testament on the doctrine of Divine Love—probably the major aspect of the movement—and her brief poem on it is one of the most familiar in Sufi literature:

Two ways I love Thee: selfishly,
And next, as worthy is of Thee.
'Tis selfish love that I do naught
Save think on thee with every thought.

'Tis purest love when Thou dost raise
The veil to my adoring gaze.
Not mine the praise in that or this:
Thine is the praise in both, I wis.

Like Rabi'a, Abu Yazid al-Bistami, mentioned earlier, had numerous followers. In so far as is known, he wrote nothing and what we have of his thought is derived from the word of mouth recorded by those followers. Al-Bastami believed that he had become God—or, as one writer on Islamic mysticism suggests, that God had become him. His acknowledgment that "When I came to the end, I saw that He had remembered me before ever I remembered Him, that He knew me before ever I knew Him, He loved me before ever I loved Him, and He had sought me before ever I went looking for Him" is one of the most arresting in all of Sufism.

Somewhat later, al-Junaid (died 910), one of the most celebrated and original of Sufi teachers, attempted a definition of Sufism which, perhaps, comes as close as any to embodying the Sufi's view of himself in relation to God. It meant, he said, that "God should cause thee to die from thyself and to live in Him." It did not mean that the mystic himself ceased to exist, rather that his individuality, a gift of God, was perfected and eternalized. Yet, man remained apart from God, ever in quest of Him. In terms reminiscent of John of the Cross several centuries later, al-Junaid saw the Sufi as a lover, searching, yearning, for his Beloved:

Though from my gaze profound
Deep awe hath hid Thy Face,
In wondrous and ecstatic Grace
I feel Thee touch my inmost ground.

But parallels can be extended too far. Elmer O'Brien, S.J., writes, in his *Varieties of Mystic Experience,* that "Sufism as the way to mystical union was initiated and sustained by the practice of a technique strikingly similar to the Jesus Prayer," and this surely is true. Nonetheless, although Islamic mysticism, like Christian and Judaic and unlike Hindu or Buddhist, makes frequent references to the idea of God and the soul, its "methods" and "techniques"—for mysticism in whatever form possesses them—and often its attitudes, differ appreciably from those of the Judaeo-Christian tradition. A degree of pantheism is, of course, one of those differences, a greater absorption in the sensuous—in, for instance, Love compared with wine, and God as the Supreme Beauty and object of all true love, another.

So, both differences and similarities there are. And, although it seems unlikely that Sufism will ever exert any powerful influence in the West, it would be difficult indeed to believe that a religion that suggests "Man is the link between God and Nature. . . . The spirit is man's real nature and within him is the secret shrine of the Divine Spirit" does not have a great deal to say to men who, perhaps most of all, have finally come to realize that they must provide, not break, that link.

THE SECRET SHRINE

A madman stood
In the middle of town.
Thousands were going and coming
To and fro on all sides.
He shouted:
"Going in a hundred directions
How can you get anywhere?
You have a single heart
But many and many a heart's desire."
—Attar of Neishapur

It is the vision of the heart that is of value, not the speech of the tongue. The true spirit is he who fears the majesty of God and frees himself from carnal desires. Until you empty yourself of self, you will not be able to escape from it. If you wish that God should dwell in your heart, purify your heart from all save Him, for the King will not enter a house filled with stores and furniture. He will only enter a heart which is empty of all save Himself and which does not admit yourself with Him.

—Abu Sa'id b. Abi 'l-Khair

O my God, who is more merciful than Yourself to all my shortcomings, for You have created me weak? And who is more forgiving than You, for Your knowledge of me was before I was? Your command to me is all-encompassing: I have resisted You only by Your permission, and You have reproached me with it; I have disobeyed You, and You were aware of it and have proved me in the wrong. I ask You for the mercy that I need and the acceptance of my pleading. For I am poor towards You, and You are bounteous towards me.

—Dhu 'l-Nun

Sell this present world of yours for the next world and you will gain both in entirety, but do not sell the next world for this world, for so shall you lose the two together. Act towards this world as if it were not, and towards the world to come as if it would never cease to be. He is a wise man who regards this world as nothing, and so regarding it, seeks the other world, instead of setting at nought the other world and seeking this. Whoso knows God regards Him as a friend and who knows this world regards Him as an enemy.

—Hasan al-Basri

O God, I never hearken to the voices of the beasts or the rustle of the trees, the splashing of waters or the song of birds, the whistling of the wind or the rumble of thunder, but I sense in them a testimony to Thy Unity and a proof of Thy Incomparableness; that Thou art the All-prevailing, the All-knowing, the All-wise, the All-just, the All-true, and that in Thee is neither overthrow nor ignorance nor folly nor injustice nor lying. O God, I acknowledge Thee in the proof of Thy handiwork and the evidence of Thy acts. Grant me, O God, to seek Thy satisfaction with my satisfaction, and the Delight of a Father in His child, remembering Thee in my love for Thee, with serene tranquility and firm resolve.

—Dhu 'l-Nun

If a person goes after more worldly possessions than he needs, he will find out that each engagement engenders another one, on and on, and here and there, indefinitely.
—Mohammad Ghazali

Love is of two natures, the love which is tranquil, which is found among both the elect and the common folk, and the love which is rapture, which is found only among the elect. This is the road which leads direct to God. Therein is found no vision of the self or the creaturely, nor any vision of motives or of states, but the lover is absorbed in the vision of God and what is from Him.

The meaning of union is that the heart should be separated from all save God and should glorify none save Him and hearken to none save Him. It means the heart's attachment to the state in which it is occupied by the glory of the One to the exclusion of all else.

—Abu Bakr al-Kalabadhi

Patience has three stages: first, it means that the servant ceases to complain, and this is the stage of repentance; second, he becomes satisfied with what is decreed, and this is the rank of the ascetics; third, he comes to love whatever his Lord does with him and this is the stage of the true friends of God. The beginning of asceticism is concern in the soul for the next world and then the coming into existence of the sweetness of hope in God. And concern for the next world does not enter in until concern for this world goes out, nor does the sweetness of hope enter in until the sweetness of desire has departed.

—Abu Talib al-Makki

Beware of this world, for its hopes are lies, its expectations false; its easefulness is all harshness, muddied its limpidity. And therein thou are in peril. . . . Hard is the life of a man if he be prudent, dangerous if comfortable, being wary ever of catastrophe, certain of his ultimate fate. Even had the Almighty not pronounced upon the world at all, nor coined for it any similitude, nor charged me to abstain from it, yet would the world itself have awakened the slumberer, and roused the heedless; how much the more then, seeing that God has Himself sent us a warning against it, an exhortation regarding it! For this world has neither worth nor weight with God; so slight it is, it weighs not with God so much as a pebble or a single clod of earth.

—Hasan al-Basri

The whole world is a marketplace for Love,
For naught that is, from Love remains remote.
The Eternal Wisdom made all things in Love:
On Love they all depend, to Love all turn.
The earth, the heavens, the sun, the moon,
    the stars
The center of their orbit find in Love.
By Love are all bewildered, stupefied,
Intoxicated by the Wine of Love.
From each, a mystic silence Love demands,
What do all seek so earnestly? 'Tis Love.
Love is the subject of their inmost thoughts,
In Love no longer "Thou" and "I" exist,
For self has passed away in the Beloved.
Now will I draw aside the veil from Love,
And in the temple of mine inmost soul
Behold the Friend, Incomparable Love,
He who would know the secret of both worlds
Will find the secret of them both is Love.
              —Farid al-Din 'Attar

With two loves have I loved You,
　With a love that is selfish
　And a love that is worthy of You:

In the love that is selfish
　I busy myself with You
　And others exclude.

In the love that is worthy of You
　You raise the veil
　That I may see.

Yet not to me is the praise in this or that,
But, in that and this, is the praise to You.
　　O Beloved of hearts
　　I have no other like You.
Pity then this day this sinner that comes
　　　to You.

　My Hope,
　My Rest,
　My Delight,
The heart can love no other than only You.
　　　　　—Rabi'a al-'Adawiya

Withersoever ye turn,
there is the face of God.

—Koran

Love whispered in my ear:
Better be game
Than a hunter.
Adopt ignorance and roam free.
Give up the thought
Of becoming the sun.
Be a particle.
The horseshoes of this world
Are nailed upside down.

—Jalal al-Din Rumi

All beauty is loved by the one who is able to perceive beauty, for the perception of beauty is a delight in itself, which is loved for its own sake, not for anything else. Beautiful forms may be loved for themselves and not for any end to be obtained from them, and that cannot be denied. For instance, green things and running water are loved for themselves, not for the sake of drinking the water or eating the green things. So, too, with the blossom and the flowers and the birds, with their fair colors and beautiful forms and their perfectly symmetrical forms, the very sight of them is a joy in itself and all joy is loved. It cannot be denied that where Beauty is perceived it is natural to love it and if it is certain that God is Beauty, He must be loved by that one to whom His Beauty and His Majesty are revealed. In God and in Him alone are all these causes of love combined and it is to Him that man owes his very existence and the qualities by which he may attain to his perfection. He is the only real Benefactor and the Ultimate Cause of all benefits. If, where beauty is found, it is natural to love it, and if beauty consists in perfection, then it follows that the All-Beautiful, Who is Absolute Perfection, must be loved by those to whom His nature and attributes are revealed.
—Abu Hamid al-Ghazali

Verily God will say on the Day of Judgment, "O children of Adam! I was sick and ye did not visit Me." And the sons of Adam will say, "O our defender, how could we visit Thee? For Thou art the Lord of the universe, and art free from sickness." And God will say, "O men! such a one was sick and you did not visit him." And God will say, "O children of Adam, I asked you for food, and ye gave it Me not." And the children of Adam will say, "O our patron, how could we give Thee food, seeing Thou art the cherisher of the universe and art free from hunger and eating?" And God will say, "Such a one asked you for bread and you did not give it to him."

—Muhammad

Just as he who dies the death of the body loses all his attributes, both those worthy of praise and those worthy of condemnation alike, so in the spiritual death all attributes, both those worthy of praise and those to be condemned, come to an end, and in all the man's states what is Divine comes to take the place of what was mortal. Thus, instead of his own essence, there is the essence of God and in place of his own qualities there are the attributes of God. He who knows himself sees his whole existence to be the Divine existence, but does not realize that any change has taken place in his own nature or qualities. For when you know yourself your "I-ness" vanishes and you know that you and God are one and the same.

—Ibn al-Arabi

There are people in this world who become forgetful of themselves and their reason for being here. Their example is analogous to the pilgrim who on his way to Mecca stops at an oasis, tends to his camel, selects choice grass to feed it with, cools its drinking water with ice. He gets so busy with these things that the caravan leaves him behind and he doesn't notice it; he even forgets the object of his journey.

The wise pilgrim gives his camel the attention it needs and no more, for his heart is set on Mecca and the pilgrimage.

—Mohammad Ghazali

The Chamberlain replied: "O you whose minds and hearts are troubled, whether you exist or do not exist in the universe, the King has his being always and eternally. Thousands of worlds of creatures are no more than an ant at his gate. You bring nothing but moans and lamentations. Return then to whence you came, O vile handful of earth!"

At this, the birds were petrified with astonishment. Nevertheless, when they came to themselves a little, they said: "Will this great king reject us so ignominiously? And if he really has this attitude to us may he not change it to one of honor? Remember Majnun who said, "If all the people who dwell on earth wished to sing my praises, I would not accept them; I would rather have the insults of Laila. One of her insults is more to me than a hundred compliments from another woman!"

"The lightning of his glory manifests itself," said the Chamberlain, "and it lifts up the reason of all souls. What benefit is there if the soul be consumed by a hundred sorrows? What benefit is there at this moment in either greatness or littleness?"

The birds, on fire with love, said: "How can the moth save itself from the flame when it wishes to be one with the flame? The friend we seek will content us by allowing us to be united to him. If now we are refused, what is there left for us to do? We are like the moth who wished for union with the flame of the candle. They begged him not to sacrifice himself so foolishly and for such an impossible aim, but he thanked them for their advice and told them that since his heart was given to the flame for ever, nothing else mattered."

—Farid al-Din 'Attar

Man is the link between God and Nature. Every man is a copy of God in His perfection; none is without the power to become a perfect man. It is the Holy Spirit which witnesses to man's innate perfection, the spirit is man's real nature and within him is the secret shrine of the Divine Spirit. As God has descended into man, so man must ascend to God, and in the Perfect Man, the true saint, the Absolute Being, which had descended from its Absoluteness, return again unto itself.

—'Abd al-Karim Jili

When you see a person who has been given
more than you in money and beauty then look
to those who have been given less.
                                    —Muhammad

O Lord, from Whom all good is hoped for, and Who art sought out in all afflictions and from Whom men seek the fulfillment of every need: from Thee they seek the generous forgiveness of every guilty deed and Thy pity. Thou knowest all things which we know not and Thou seest all things, which we cannot do, as Thou discernest what is secret and dost look into the consciences of Thy creation. Thou has power over all things.

Because of what I have found of the flowing forth of Thy love and the fragrance of Thy proximity, I feel contempt for the firm mountains and the earth and the heavens. If Thou wert to offer to sell me Paradise for a moment of my time with Thee, or for one moment of the least of my spiritual states, I would not buy it. If Thou wert to place before me Hellfire, with all it contains of torment, I would think lightly of it in comparison with my state when Thou art hidden from me. Forgive the people and do not forgive me, and have mercy upon them and do not have mercy upon me. I do not intercede with Thee for myself nor beseech Thee for what is due to me. Do with me what Thou wilt.

—Husayn b. Mansur al-Hallaj

You ought to know yourself as you really are, so that you may understand of what nature you are and whence you have come to this world and for what purpose you were created and in what your happiness and misery consist. For within you are combined the qualities of the animals and the wild beasts and also the qualities of the angels, but the spirit is your real essence, and all beside it is, in fact, foreign to you. So strive for knowledge of your origin so that you may know how to attain to the Divine Presence and the contemplation of the Divine majesty and beauty, and deliver yourself from the fetters of lust and passion. For God did not create you to be their captive, but that they should be your thralls, under your control, for the journey which is before you, to be your steed and your weapon, so that you may therewith pursue your happiness, and when you have no more need of them, then cast them under your feet.

—Abu Hamid al-Ghazali

Gratitude is the vision of the Giver, not of the gift. It comes from God Himself. Hope and fear are like the two wings of a bird, when it is flying straight to its destination: If one wing fails, its flight fails and if both fail, it dies. Hope is the vision of God in His perfect Beauty.

The Divine revelation which comes to those who are waiting in expectation for it comes like flashes of lightning, then like rays of light, and then the light in its full splendor.
—Abu 'l-Qasim al-Qushairi

Creatures are subject to "states," but the gnostic has no "state," because his vestiges are effaced and his essence is annihilated by the essence of another and his traces are lost in another's traces.

I went from God to God, until they cried from me in me, "O thou I!"—i.e., I attained the stage of annihilation in God.

Nothing is better for man than to be without aught, having no asceticism, no theory, no practice. When he is without all he is with all.

. . . They asked [Bistami], "When does a man know that he has attained real gnosis?" He said: "At the time when he becomes annihilated under the knowledge of God and is made everlasting on the carpet of God, without self and without creature."

—Abu Yazid al-Bistami

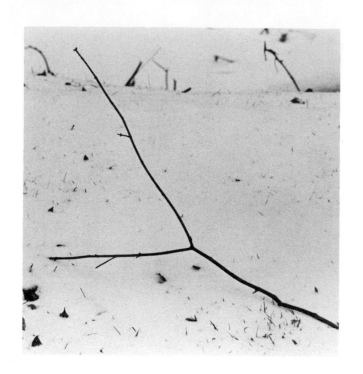

Meekness and shame are two branches of faith and vain talking and embellishing are two branches of hypocrisy.

—Muhammad

I have not served God from fear of Hell; I would be a wretched hireling if I served Him from fear. Nor have I served Him from the desire for Paradise; I would be a bad servant if I served for the sake of what was given to me. I have served Him only because I love Him and desire Him.

—Rabi'a al-'Adawiya

The wise men and the sages are idle and carefree; they reap the harvest without ploughing. God does their work for them. People don't see God's work, so they sweat and fret, hustle and beg from morning till night.
—Jalal al-Din Rumi

Acquire knowledge. It enableth its possessor to distinguish right from wrong; it lighteth the way to Heaven; it is our friend in the desert, our society in solitude, our companion when friendless; it guideth us to happiness; it sustaineth us in misery; it is an ornament amongst friends and an armor against enemies.

—Muhammad

When a fly is plunged in honey, all the members of its body are reduced to the same condition, and it does not move. Similarly the term "absorption in God" is applied to one who has no conscious existence or initiative or movement. Any action that proceeds from him is not his own. If he is still struggling in the water, or if he cries out, "Oh, I am drowning," he is not said to be in the state of absorption. This is what is signified by the words *Ana 'l-Haqq* ("I am God"). People imagine that it is a presumptuous claim, whereas it is really a presumptuous claim to say *Ana 'l-'abd* ("I am the slave of God"); and *Ana 'l-Haqq* ("I am God") is an expression of great humility. The man who says *Ana 'l-'abd* affirms two existences, his own and God's, but he that says *Ana 'l-Haqq* ("I am God") has made himself non-existent and has given himself up and says "I am God," i.e., "I am naught, He is all: there is no being but God's." This is the extreme of humility and self-abasement.

—Jalal al-Din Rumi

There is no existence save His existence. To this the Prophet pointed when he said: "Revile not the world, for God is the world," pointing to the fact that the existence of the world is God's existence without partner or like or equal. It is related that the Prophet declared that God said to Moses: "O My servant, I was sick and thou didst not visit Me: I asked help of thee and thou didst not give it to Me," and other like expressions. This means that the existence of the beggar is His existence and the existence of the sick is His existence. Now when this is admitted, it is acknowledged that this existence is His existence and that the existence of all created things, both accidents and substances, is His existence, and when the secret of one atom of the atoms is clear, the secret of all created things, both outward and inward, is clear, and you do not see in this world or the next anything except God, for the existence of these two abodes and their name, and what they name, all of them are assuredly He.

—Ibn al-Arabi

Happy was I
In the pearl's heart to lie;
Till, lashed by life's hurricane,
Like a tossed wave I ran.

The secret of the sea
I uttered thunderously;
Like a spent cloud on the shore
I slept, and stirred no more.

—Jalal al-Din Rumi

Know that everything is vanity except God.
　　　　　　　　　　　　　　—Lebid

Thou, Whose breath is sweetest perfume to
 the spent and anguished heart,
Thy remembrance to Thy lovers bringeth
 ease for every smart.
Multitudes like Moses, reeling, cry to earth's
 remotest place:
"Give me sight, O Lord!" they clamor,
 seeking to behold Thy face.
Multitudes no man has numbered, lovers,
 and afflicted all,
Stumbling on the way of anguish, "Allah!
 Allah!" loudly call.
And the fire of separation sears the heart and
 burns the breast,
And their eyes are wet with weeping for a
 love that gives not rest.
"Poverty's my pride"—Thy lovers raise to
 heav'n their battle-cry,
Gladly meeting men's derision, letting all the
 world go by.
      —'Abd Allah al-Ansari

O God, seek me out of Thy mercy that I may come to Thee; and draw me on with Thy Grace that I may turn to Thee.

O God, I shall never lose all hope of Thee even though I disobey Thee; and I shall never cease to fear Thee even though I obey Thee.

O God, the very worlds have themselves driven me unto Thee, and my knowledge of Thy bounty has brought me to stand before Thee.

O God, how shall I be disappointed seeing that Thou art my hope; or how shall I be despised seeing that in Thee is my trust?

O Thou Who art veiled in the shrouds of Thy glory, so that no eye can perceive Thee! O Thou Who shinest forth in the perfection of Thy splendor, so that the hearts [of the mystics] have realized Thy majesty! How shall Thou be hidden, seeing that Thou art ever present, and watchest over us?

—Ibn 'Ata' Allah

When God created the earth, it began to shake and tremble; then God created mountains and put them upon the earth, and the land became firm and fixed; and the angels were astonished at the hardness of the hills and said, "O God, is there anything of Thy creation stronger than hills?" And God said, "Yes, water is stronger than the hills, because it breaketh them." Then the angels said, "O Lord, is there anything of Thy creation stronger than water?" He said, "Yes, wind overcometh water: it doth agitate it and put it in motion." They said, "O our Lord! is there anything of Thy creation stronger than wind?" He said, "Yes, the children of Adam giving alms: those who give with their right hand, and conceal from their left, overcome all."

—Muhammad

I was mistaken in four different ways. I made it my concern to remember God, to know Him, to love Him, and to seek Him. And when I came to the end, I saw that He had remembered me before ever I remembered Him, that He knew me before ever I knew Him, He loved me before ever I loved Him, and He had sought me before ever I went looking for Him.

—Abu Yazid al-Bistami

By love bitter things are made sweet; copper turns to gold. By love, the sediment becomes clear; by love torment is removed. By love the dead is made to live; by love the sovereign is made a slave. This love also is the fruit of knowledge. When did folly sit on a throne like this? The faith of love is separated from all religion. For lovers the faith and the religion is God. O spirit, in striving and seeking, become like running water. O reason, at all times be ready to give up mortality for the sake of immortality. Remember God always, that self may be forgotten, so that your self may be effaced in the One to Whom you pray, without care for who is praying, or the prayer.

—Jalal al-Din Rumi

To those who love Thee, there is no difference between monastery and tavern, for everywhere shines the light of the face of the Beloved. Wherever glory is given to Thee in a place where Thou art worshipped, the bell which summons men to prayer, and the cloister and the monk and the name of the Cross, all serve one purpose. What lover of God is there whose state is not regarded by the Beloved? O sir, there is no pain for you in this, and if it should be otherwise, there is a Physician Who can heal you.

—Shams al-Din Hafiz

A bumptious man dismissed a dervish by shouting at him: "Nobody knows you here."

"But I know myself," the dervish replied. "How sad it would be if the reverse were true."

—Attar of Neishapur

The life of this world is but a sport, and a play, and a gaud, something to boast about among yourselves.

—Koran

All that we behold and perceive by our senses bears undeniable witness to the existence of God and His power and His knowledge and the rest of His attributes, whether these things be manifested or hidden, the stone and the clod, the plants and trees, the living creatures, the heavens and the earth and the stars, the dry land and the ocean, the fire and the air,

substance and accident; and indeed we our-
selves are the chief witness to Him. But just
as the bat sees only at night, when the light
is veiled by darkness, and cannot therefore
see in the daytime, because of the weakness
of its sight, which is dazzled by the full light
of the sun, so also the human mind is too weak
to behold the full glory of the Divine majesty.
                        —Abu Hamid al-Ghazali

Everything upon the earth passeth away, save His face.

—Koran

A man came before the Prophet with a carpet and said, "O Prophet! I passed through a wood and heard the voices of the young birds; and I took and put them into my carpet; and their mother came fluttering round my head and I uncovered them, and the mother fell down upon them; then I wrapped them up in my carpet again; and there are the young which I have." Then the Prophet said, "Put them down." And when he did so, their mother joined them, and the Prophet said, "Do you wonder at the affection of the mother towards her young? I swear by Him who hath sent me, verily God is more loving to His servants than the mother to these young birds. Return them to the place from which ye took them, and let their mother be with them."

—Muhammad

Last night I vowed anew, I swore an oath by your life,

That I would never remove my eyes from your face; if You smite with the sword, I will not turn from You.

I will not seek the cure from any other, because my pain is of separation from You.

If you should cast me into the fire, I am no true man if I utter a sigh.

I rose from your path like dust; now I return to the dust of your path.

—Jalal al-Din Rumi

The heart is like a grain of corn, we are like a mill; how does the mill know why this turning?

The body is like a stone, and the water its thoughts; the stone says, "The water knows what is toward."

The water says, "Ask the miller, for it was he who flung this water down."

The miller says to you, "Bread-eater, if this does not turn, how shall the crumb-broth be?"

Much business is in the making; silence, ask God, that He may tell you.

—Jalal al-Din Rumi

I have bestowed on everyone a particular
mode of worship, I have given everyone a
peculiar form of expression.
The idiom of Hindustan is excellent for
Hindus; the idiom of Sind is excellent for
the people of Sind.
I look not at tongues and speech, I look at the
spirit and the inward feeling.
I look into the heart to see whether it be
lowly, though the words uttered be not
lowly.
Enough of phrases and conceits and
metaphors! I want burning, burning:
become familiar with that burning!
Light up a fire of love in thy soul, burn all
thought and expression away!
O Moses, they that know the conventions
are of one sort, they whose souls burn
are of another.

The religion of love is apart from all religions.
The lovers of God have no religion but
God alone.
—Jalal al-Din Rumi

Be in a domain where neither good nor evil exists: both of them belong to the world of created things; in the presence of Unity there is neither command nor prohibition.

All this talk and turmoil and noise and movement is outside of the veil; within the veil is silence and calm and rest.

Dost thou hear how there comes a voice from the brooks of running water? But when they reach the sea they are quiet, and the sea is neither augmented by their incoming nor diminished by their outgoing.

—Abu Yazid al-Bistami

I die, and yet not dies in me
The ardor of my love for Thee,
Nor hath Thy Love, my only goal,
Assuaged the fever of my soul.

To Thee alone my spirit cries;
In Thee my whole ambition lies,
And still Thy wealth is far above
The poverty of my small love.

I turn to Thee in my request,
And seek in Thee my final rest;
To Thee my loud lament is brought,
Thou dwellest in my secret thought.

However long my sickness be,
This wearisome infirmity,
Never to men will I declare
The burden Thou hast made me bear.

To Thee alone is manifest
The heavy labor of my breast,
Else never kin nor neighbors know
The brimming measure of my woe.

A fever burns below my heart
And ravages my every part;
It hath destroyed my strength and stay,
And smoldered all my soul away.

Guidest Thou not upon the road
The rider wearied by his load,
Delivering from the steeps of death
The traveller as he wandereth?

Didst Thou not light a beacon too
For them that found the guidance true
But carried not within their hand
The faintest glimmer of its brand?

O then to me Thy favor give
That, so attended, I may live,
And overwhelm with ease from Thee
The rigor of my poverty.
                              —Dhu 'l-Nun

I would be ashamed to ask for the things of the world from Him to whom the world belongs. How then can I ask for them from those to whom it does not belong?

—Rabi'a al-'Adawiya

The sea
Will be a sea
Whatever the drop's philosophy.
—Attar of Neishapur

Mortals, like water-birds, are born of the sea of spirit. Why should a bird who has risen from that sea make his abode in this place? But we are pearls in this sea, all of us have our place in it. Otherwise why should wave after wave come from the sea of spirit? It is the opportunity for us to attain union, the time to reach the beauty of immortality, the time to draw near and receive gifts, it is the ocean of perfect purity. The wave of gifts has appeared, the Throne of God has risen from the sea, the dawn of happiness has appeared. Is it the dawn? Nay, it is the light of God. God's light gives radiance to the light of sense. That is the meaning of Light upon light. The light of the senses draws us towards the earth. The Light of God draws us up on high.

—Jalal al-Din Rumi

What excuses have you to offer, my heart, for so many shortcomings? Such constancy on the part of the Beloved, such unfaithfulness on your own?

So much generosity on his side, on yours such niggling contrariness! So many graces from him, so many faults committed by you!

Such envy, such evil imaginings and dark thoughts in your heart, such drawing, such tasting, such munificence by him!

Why all this tasting? That your bitter soul may become sweet. Why all this drawing? That you may join the company of the saints.

—Jalal al-Din Rumi

If men wish to draw near to God, they must seek Him in the hearts of men. They should speak well of all men, whether present or absent, and if they themselves seek to be a light to guide others, then, like the sun, they must show the same face to all. To bring joy to a single heart is better than to build many shrines for worship, and to enslave one soul by kindness is worth more than the setting free of a thousand slaves.

That is the true man of God, who sits in the midst of his fellowmen, and rises up and eats and sleeps and buys and sells and gives and takes in the bazaars amongst other people, and who marries and has social intercourse with other folk, and yet is never for one moment forgetful of God.

—Abu Sa'id b. Abi 'l-Khair

One night the poet Awhadi of Kerman was sitting on his porch, bent over a vessel. Shams-e Tabrizi happened to pass by.

    Shams: "What are you doing?"

    Awhadi: "Contemplating the moon in a bowl of water."

    Shams: "Unless you have broken your neck, why don't you look at the moon in the sky?"

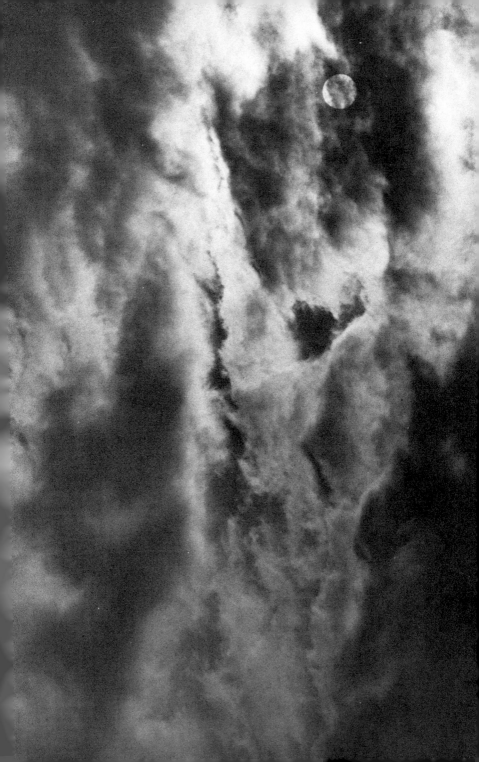

If you look into muddy water, you see neither the moon nor the sky; sun and moon both disappear when darkness possesses the air.

—Jalal al-Din Rumi

How should not I mourn, like night,
        without His day and the favor of
        His day-illuming
                countenance?

His unsweetness is sweet to my
        soul: may my soul be sacrificed
                to the Beloved who grieves
                my heart!

I am in love with grief and pain for
        the sake of pleasing my
                peerless King.

Tears shed for His sake are pearls,
        though people think they
                are tears.

I complain of the Soul of my soul,
        But in truth I am not
                complaining: I am only
                telling.

My heart says it is tormented by
        Him, and I have long been
                laughing at its poor
                pretense.

Do me right, O Glory of the
 righteous, O Thou Who art the
  dais, and I the threshold
   of Thy door!

Where are threshold and dais in
 reality? Where the Beloved is,
  where are "we" and "I"?

O Thou Whose soul is free from
 "we" and "I," O Thou Who art
  the essence of the spirit in
   men and women,

When men and women become one,
 Thou art that One; when the
  units are wiped out, lo,
   Thou art that Unity.

Thou didst contrive this "I" and
 "we" in order to play the game
  of worship with Thyself,

That all "I's" and "thou's" might
 become one soul and at last be
  submerged in the Beloved.
   —Jalal al-Din Rumi

A lover knocked at the door of his beloved.

"Who is it?"

"It is I."

"Go away. This house will not hold you and I."

The rejected lover retreated into the wilderness. For a long time he prayed and meditated on the beloved's words. Finally he returned and knocked at the door again.

"Who is it?"

"It is you."

Immediately the door opened.

—Attar of Neishapur

"Assuredly in the creation of the heavens and of the earth; and in the alternation of night and day; and in the ships which pass through the seas with things useful to man; and in the rain which God sendeth down from Heaven, giving life thereby to the earth after it was dead, scattering over it all manner of cattle; and in the change of the winds, and in the clouds that are made to do service between the Heaven and the earth; in all these things are signs for those who understand. . . . Verily God is not ashamed to set forth as well the instance of a gnat."

—Koran

I have seen nothing more conducive to righteousness than solitude, for he who is alone sees nothing but God, and if he sees nothing but God, nothing moves him but the will of God.

Every intercessor is veiled by his intercessions from contemplation of the Truth, for the Truth is present to the people of faith, since God Himself is the Creative Truth and His word is Truth and there is no need for anyone to make intercession, when God Himself is present with him and manifested to him. If he were absent, then should intercession be made to Him.

—Dhu 'l-Nun

Plug thy low sensual ear, which stuffs
    like cotton
Thy conscience and makes deaf thine
    inward ear.
Be without ear, without sense, without
    thought,
And hearken to the call of God, "Return!"
Our speech and action is the outer journey,
Our inner journey is above the sky
The body travels on its dusty way;
The spirit walks, like Jesus, on the sea.

—Jalal al-Din Rumi

O Generous, who bounty givest!
O Wise, Who sins forgivest!
O Eternal, Who to our sense comest not near!
O One, Who art in essence and quality
          without peer!
O Powerful, Who of Godhead worthy art!
O Creator, who shewest the way to every
          erring heart!
To my soul give Thou of Thy Own
          spotlessness,
And to my eyes of Thy Own luminousness;
And unto us, of Thy bounty and goodness,
          whatever may be best
Make Thou that Thy bequest.

O Lord, in mercy grant my soul to live,
And patience grant, that hurt I may
          not grieve:
    How shall I know what thing is best
          to seek?
Thou only knowest: what Thou knowest,
          give!

          —'Abd Allah al-Ansari

Beware of this world with all wariness; for it is like to a snake, smooth to the touch, but its venom is deadly. Turn away from whatsoever delights thee in it, for the little companioning thou wilt have of it; put off from thee its cares, for that thou hast seen its sudden chances, and knowest for sure that thou shalt be parted from it; endure firmly its hardships, for the ease that shall presently be thine. The more it pleases thee, the more do thou be wary of it; for the man of this world, whenever he feels secure in any pleasures thereof, the world drives him over into some unpleasantness, and whenever he attains any part of it and squats him down upon it, the world suddenly turns him upside down.

—Hasan al-Basri

When the unveiling of the Divine glory is given to anyone, his existence becomes a burden to him and all his attributes a source of reproach to him. He who belongs to God and to whom God belongs has no concern with anything else. The real meaning of gnosis [knowledge] is to know that the Kingdom is God's. When anyone knows that all power is in the hand of God, what further concern has he with the creatures, that he should be veiled from God, by himself or them? All veils come from ignorance; when ignorance has passed away, the veils vanish and this life, by means of gnosis, becomes one with the life to come.

—Abu 'l-Hasan al-Jullabi al-Hujwiri

At the night prayer, when the sun declines to sinking, this way of the senses is closed and the way to the Unseen is opened.

The angel of sleep then drives forward the spirits, even as the shepherd who watches over his flock.

To the placeless, towards the spiritual meadows, what cities and what gardens he there displays to them!

The spirit beholds a thousand marvelous forms and shapes, when sleep excises from it the image of the world.

You might say that the spirit was always a dweller there, it remembers not this world, and its weariness does not increase.

Its heart so escapes from the load and burden for which it trembled here, that no care for it gnaws at it any more.

—Jalal al-Din Rumi

Out of all the world I chose you alone; do you deem it right for me to sit sorrowful?

My heart is like a pen in your hand; through you it is, whether I am glad or grieve.

What shall I be other than what you wish? What shall I see except what you show?

Now you cause thorns to grow from me, now roses; now I smell roses, now I pluck thorns.

Since you keep me so, I am so—since you wish me so, I am so.

In that vat where you dispense dye to the heart, what should I be? What my love and hate?

You were the first, and you will be the last: do you make my last better than my first.

When you are hidden, I am of the infidels; when you appear, I am of the faithful.

What do I possess other than the thing you have given? What are you searching for in my pocket and sleeve?

—Jalal al-Din Rumi

Love resides not in science and learning, scrolls and pages; whatever men chatter about, that way is not the lovers' way.

Know that the branch of Love is in pre-eternity and its roots in post-eternity; this tree rests not upon heaven and earth, upon legs.

We have deposed reason and circumscribed passion, for such majesty is not appropriate to this reason and these habits.

So long as you are desirous, know that this desire of yours is an idol; when you have become beloved, after that there is no existence for the desirous.

The mariner is always upon the planks of fear and hope; once planks and mariner have passed away, nothing remains but drowning.

Shams-i Tabrizi, you are at once sea and pearl, for your being entirely is naught but the secret of the Creator.

—Jalal al-Din Rumi

I sought a soul in the sea,
And found a coral there;
Beneath the foam for me
An ocean was all laid bare.

Into my heart's night
Along a narrow way
I groped; and lo! the light,
An infinite land of day.
                    —Jalal al-Din Rumi